# Spirals and Circles

# Spirals and Circles

## A Collection of Poems
## by

### Matt Seigne

Printed by:
ProPrint
Riverside Cottage
Old Great North Road
Stibbington
PE8 6LR

# Contents

## *Flow On*

The sky last night
was a beautiful sight
I saw the stars
and the moon
shining bright
this mothership sailing
thru space
flowing on
at its own pace.

Solar temple
21st June
the light from the sun
just played on you
local forest
December 24
the light from the moon
was your own torch.

Flow on
Mother Earth
you had your own way here
you had your own birth
flow on
Father Sun
shine yeah gifted
beautiful one!

## Pure Rock Art

Walked into the stone circle
found a mystery there
Pure rock art
from an age we don't know
or perhaps we do?

Spirals and circles
kinky patterns too
all made as beautiful signs
to show them through.


## The Ladybird

Happy is the ladybird
as she spots a stable leaf
enjoying for a while
this quiet little piece.

Happy is the ladybird
as she whizzes through the trees
enjoying for a time
this quiet little peace.

## Star Struck

A curtain of clouds
hangs above the stage of the hills.
There comes the first appearance
of the great performer –
the golden sun.

The golden sun smiles on
through the valley
and the audience of trees
sways to the rhythm
of the breeze.


## Into is Shone

We looked into the stars
and saw a million miles
and realised everything's always new.
We looked to the sun
and saw all our friends
and realised they never went away
we glanced into each other's eyes
only truth never lies
there we found a million stars again.

## S.P.R.I.N.G.

Pink purple orange green
in spring nature's like a high speed train
buzzing with life
no stopping the spring
makes you wake up
to its love within.

Peach white yellow cream
everyone different
everything scene
cruisin' the cosmic
on this spinning thing
takes you right up
to its love within.


## Snail

Snail
small
spiral shell
in this mini-forest

Snail
glide
subtle hide
in this natural florist.

## Golden Sea

You
for me
are a golden sea
of glittering shiny
water

In your depths
no regrets
just glowing
lost treasure

In your palms
1000 calms
one for every weather

In your breast
the very best
a landscape
fit forever!

In between your toes
1000 coves
one for every pleasure
life's a peach
on your beach
a shoreline
without measure.

## The Uni-Verse

Yesterday it was tomorrow
now it's today
the way we weave
the way we play
now and again
and then again
we reach up high
bringing down to us
some beautiful sky.

## The First Circle

When the first circle
appeared on his land
he didn't tell anyone
not one living man
he didn't know what he'd found
he doesn't know today
I guess he feels some mystery at play?!

It was the first circle
that laid the crops down
not one ear damaged
not one footstep around
it was the first circle
he saw on his land
appearing untouched
by anyone else's hand.

It was the first circle
from a long time ago
that fuels the explosion
we now know -
every seed planted
every single year
may get the chance
to appear!

# Evening

Wind so fresh
kiss my hair
sky so blue
just being there
friend so cool
I am aware!
I put aside
my work that's done
it's time now
to have some
candles lit
fire burn
read the Celts
and learn!

# The Coombes

Tree so bare
silhouette branch
curved
beautiful
the sun rise
the morning mist.

## Open Heart Sanctuary

When you tell me
something's missing
and you have a forest heart
privileged with golden leaves
yet needing a clearing part -

If you open up our loving heart
to me
I will be the one to share
all the secrets
that you hold inside
let them flow out
let them flow right out.


## The Centre Light

As I stood in the centre light
I realised this place was right
for the people living there
long ago -
I guess if you build a monument
and praise it for its beautifulness
it blends into the scene.

Lakes and rivers and mountainsides
anywhere you wanna be alive
anywhere water gives us life!
Rice salad mushroom sauce
peanut cashew
all in awe
all in awe!

## Kristal Maize

Sometimes appearances can be deceiving
sometimes that's worth revealing.
A four thousand year old tree
is still breathing
a twelve ton block of stone
in a pyramid's ceiling.

Why you've got the answer
why you hold it in your hand!

Sometimes appearances can be misleading
sometimes that's worth revealing.
What happens on the outside
is weaving
what happens on the inside
is healing.


## Silver Moon and Many Rivers

she looks good in the sky tonight
the moon is shining down so bright.
There's an aeroplane flying across the sky
where are those people heading tonight?

Where you going tonight
is it really so far?
Where you going tonight
following beautiful stars?

I stand with my feet on the ground
listening to the silent night sound
Tonight is cool
tonight for me!
My breath in the air
is as free as can be.

# Honfleur

I put the coffee on the fire
and I breathed real deep
I picked at the pasta
that I picked up real cheap
I looked at the flames
and listened to the sound
of the nightbirds calling -
calling across the misty ground.


# Some Gratitude

I turn on the water tap
and give thanks for what I drink
I turn the pages
of a real good book
and give thanks for what I think.
Our friends all came over
and they left their shoes outside.
We talked through the evening
and partied all the night!

## Star Guide

There's a guide
that you will always answer
that's the beauty
of a love enhancer
someone who will care
no matter what
someone to help the balance of you
somewhere somehow
it will happen yet!

There's a sign
in every chance encounter
there's a message
if you care to read it
that's the beauty
of a chance encounter
someone will listen
when you least expect.

## Embracing

Beside the fire
by the water's edge
I see your face a-glowing
an orangy red
the sun and moon
have joined hands
face to face they kiss
goodnight honeywood
goodnight
good morning kiss.

## Livin' Rivers

Livin' rivers ebb and flow
until they reach sea
from the mountains
they are sprung
livin' rivers
flow right on.
And the valleys hold them
livin' rivers flow right on.


## Peak Visuals

60's architects
gained higher creativity
inventing crazy buildings
and lots of zany things
silicon valley
psychedelic valley
Microsoft
open minds
computer mirrors those
computer creators
on similar trips
some could even see
electricity running
like water in drips.

## Lunar!

Last night I awoke
to the sound of a giant moo!
the season of the calf
created this review
The puppy jumped over the bed
as the cat shot out to play
wide awake I stepped out
to see the half moon.


## In Her Peace

As she flies by with her mystical eye
waking up to see her smile!
As the east wind blows
I find a flow
I find a way to survive.

somehow she found out
she was born inside.
In this place
she plays the ace,
a joker in every rhyme.

Five hundred piece
jigsaw in her hand
she'll make the picture
and remember!
As the east wind blows
we find a flow
we find a way to revive.

## Strong Medicine

Strong medicine
the air to breathe
outside the moors
inside the tea.
After the last sip
of something Chinese
outside I slip
and release!


## The Interactive

The truest moments
for the coolest thoughts
let everything be
and everything sorts
left hand skywards
the right on the ground
flowing movements
are all in the sound.

Something you like
but you don't always know
are the beautiful ones
the ones who show?
Relaxed in the feel
you gotta be brave
but that doesn't mean
relaxing's a crave.

## Natural Springs

Friends journey from far and wide
finding centres where they eat and buy
in towns and places on energy lines
if they need to replace, recharging life.

Exchanging, borrowing, flying kites
soon days become shorter with longer nights
leaves fall and squirrels hide
rusty colours blow day and night.

A festival lights up the skies
a celebration of all our lives
then the new year brings another tide
good things sand things all in time.

Getting together to heat the days
by talking, doing and feeling ways
twinkling stars in cosmic skies
friends with drinks at firesides

Thunder snow lightning rain
seen every year but never the same
sharing the birth of another new spring
sowing the seeds growing within

Looking on colours and hearing new sounds
the latest tricks and the coolest styles
pebbles washed up at ocean's shore
fruits from trees on garden's floor

Birds sing with spirit and warmth
carrying the light natural springs forth.

## The Orange

The orange is fine
seeds and all
we're lucky to have
this fruity ball
so waxy I praise it
so try to amaze it?
You can't!
It's got it all.
Roundness and flavour
no label to its favour
it is what it is
an amazing ball!


## Water Leg

Soft like water
is Leo's leg
when I grasp it
and try to hold it
it slips through my fingers
like a trickle of water
from a mountain spring.
He is soft supple and flowing
a real feline glowing
ginger fur golden purr
cool and all-knowing.

## I Wonder

Blue cloud sky
corn stands tall
in a field
square cut
secure all round
trees sway
in the breeze
light on leaves
flutter
and just rest.


## Frequent Seas

I look to the ocean
some inspiration from a cave.
I look to a notion
that inspiration is a wave
we look to a notion
that any ocean
is a potion just like rain.

I find this emotion
to be a potion
that's not explained.
That's why we are learning
never yearning
to love we give the same.
That's the clever turning
the water churning
the flame burning.

## Cosmic Citizens

Oh when the clock chimes
there's a change in time
and when the babe cries
there's a change alright!
And when plane glides
there's a change in flight
and when the moon shines
there's a change at night.
Turnabout and turnaround
there's a change that's coming round
that's coming soon . . .

We come with peace
to share the change
we come with peace
to share the age!

## Some Alignments

Sometimes when you guess
you guess the right way
and sometimes when you guess
you get it wrong!
Sometimes when the sun rises
the clouds obscure its view
but somehow you know it's always there
I just wanna say
that every single day
has its own way of saying
hello!


## The Motion Picture

Your truth is there for you to know
you just wanna be loved
and show your glow
like a reed in a river
it bends with the flow
staying strong inside to grow.
Or like a leaf on a tree
needs to bend with the snow
staying strong inside to grow.

## Busy Being

When you seek to choose
you choose to seek
when you talk
you choose to speak.
I can see you getting stronger
in this world
I can feel you sometimes
hold a pearl.
Just busy being
just being busy
just looking after family
just not losing sight
of who you be
just giving something to you
and me.


## Simple H'art

I looked high into the sky
and realised that I am
just a little man
who walks on this earth.

I looked deep into the sea
and realised that we are
like the pebbles on the beach
just reaching in from the shore.

Yes it's good to love
it's good to learn
sometimes we wish
sometimes we yearn
but.

## Season All

When the winter comes
there's ice and snow
when the winter comes
fires glow.

Cold frosty mornings
dark evenings too
it's good to be warm
in bed with you.

When the summer comes
all the colours show
when the summer comes
those feelings flow.

Warm dusty mornings
light evenings too
it's good to be cool
cool in bed with you.

## All Friends Are

When I thought I heard you request
I gave you what I thought was best
just be calm and cool
and make your quest
to join your journey
like a bird flies its nest.
I wish you vitality
and the road is clear
smell those roses
'cause they're always near.
That famous bed
doesn't have to be high
you can sleep on the journey
take your time.

## Beautiful City

This beautiful city
it can be if you want
friends, relations and celebrations
if you want.

This anthill teaming
this beehive gleaming
this nest built by hand
weaving patterns
on its beautiful satins
enjoying every gland.

## *Flow On Too*

Sometimes I fail
and don't I know it?!
Seems like
we sometimes blow it
can't think of a time
there wasn't a doubt
situations change
they turn about

Like last weekend
I felt like a star
beautiful friends
beautiful ahh!

Clocks change
the weather moves on
fires glow
water rolls on
books change
friends move on
metal shines
crystal Earth pulses on.

## Optimystic

Last weekend I swear I saw
a beautiful thing,
a football team wearing red
getting a win!
This weekend I couldn't hope
for anything more.
But surprises round the corner
are always in store.

'Cause this weekend's gonna be
the best that I've ever had
it's gonna be the best
so good!

Somebody must love you
and the state you're in.
Looking at the stars
I see a bright one spin.
Could it be a sign that
after all I've seen
I didn't need to worry
about a single thing?!

## Dogs Must Dream

Dogs must dream
it's in their nature to find
looking for signs everywhere
to see you they can be kind.
Dogs must dream
on them you may depend
their friendship is immeasurable
you know where you are with them!


## Little Spa

Twinkle twinkle little spa
how I wonder what you are
up above the fields you flow
thru the mountains
and past the snow.

If I could sense you magical glow
I think a star would appear to show.

Simple simple little spa
you ooze the beauty
that you are,
inter-linked with everything
from plant to creature
with water you spring!

## Grasmere

C'mon riding
lakeview summer sky
the receiver is the believer
not that pie in the sky
to try
that's right!
We're turned on.


## Breakfast in Style

Waves defeat me
the sea's gone wild
Out on the beach
Breakfast in style
Second hand shop
open today
gonna get some soap
to wash those tears away!

I looked to the west
I can't decide which vest
I go out alone
looking for a phone
hit my fingers on the buttons
taking my time
out on the beach
it's everytime.

# Rural Guesthouse

Country cottage in the sun
different to the city
and so much fun
cooking food in the pot
when I taste it
it hits the spot!
Of course it's real when you're here
creation has a beautiful feel
relaxing sometimes I know it's true
the magic
the pleasure
the creaking shoes!

# The Horseshoe

Canal
bedroom window
water and sleep
Silbury Hill
and hills
with horses on.

No time for Bath
but time for some
Malvern slope
football fun!

Thank you Coventry man
and Birmingham too
someone somewhere
sometimes true.

## Global

It's a crazy f*?kin' world
s'always been
multicultural though
in fact that's only natural
a beautiful time
friends like home comforts
just fine.


## Scheep

Scheep I love you
you fluffy pearls
scheep so gentle
I can't deny
your exquisite sound
your wonderful cry!
Scheep you're common
yet un-common to us.
You watch me
and make no fuss
scheep you're naturally wild
like a tree
naturally born - forever free!

## Love Run Wild

The Romans built villas
in the countryside
the Celts built round houses
with one equal side.
In China there were
and are pyramids
harmonising with those in Egypt.

Walls are built to come down
you can't dam love
'cause love surrounds -
has no enemies
so blocked up ones
unblock yourselves
let love run!


## Anything Can Happen

Anything can happen
and anything does
Cornershop number one
thank stars above!

Anything can happen
and anything does
comedy and music
with a spirit of love.

Anything can happen
and anything does
I wrote this
for those two white doves!

## The Vibrator

Tree
forêt
le ciel bleu
le soliel brille
this morning
you do

Les vachês
the aeroplane
shudders the grass
the grass remains
and so does my arse!


## A Question of What

What's the fascination
with someone
so unhealthy
so unworldly wise?
Must be the failure
of their lies!
Or the want of love
in their earthly eyes?

## Flexible Thinkers

When it's dark we see the stars
when it's light we meet on Mars
when we feel like curling up
it's light and dark inside our cup.

Pleasing breeze blows across our faces
sand sticks in our awkward places
can you tell me what I'm facing
if I offer you a shell?

Won't you tell me nothing is wrong?
Because flexible thinkers can be anyone.
I see you and you see me
this freedom is basically
to know a friend and feel that good
even when they're misunderstood.


## Fresh Fruit

Hanging
Motionless?
Clinging
yet openness
fresh fruit.

## Rain-Rain

Rain, rain
it's wet today
the clouds have come
and gone away
rain, rain
a gentle touch
we need your juice
so very much!

Cloud, cloud
the sprinkler in the sky
amazing how you collect
when you drift so very high
cloud, cloud
you pour that stuff
the trees sway but never rust
we enjoy your gentle touch
so very much!


## Portuguese Drift

Decembro
estilo
obrigada

Decembro
estilo
obrigado

## Forest Dwelling

Siberian friend
so peaceful you
when
you're into your forest
life's life
in the forest
moving on
moving out
moving in
any way round
a Siberian mind
librarian Siberian.

## The Bats of Inner Sense

The birds are in bed
and now the bats
flutter high
silhouetted against
the deep grey sky.

The wind still blows
through the trees
bats flutter past
overhead
with such ease.

So rapid
so swooping
reputation
I don't know?
The bats this evening
caress the sky
as they come and go.

## Pulp Non-Fiction

Take out the rubbish
won't let it grow
release me of that stuff
I wanna be in flow.

Clear up that game
of Monopoly
eat the last few nuts
and switch off TV.

Pass around your photo
to another new friend
this is what it looks like
in the forest's east end.

Here's an old ticket
left in my back pocket
of when we went to see
the Star War's trilogy.

## The Witness was a Fish

Got no time to beat
you feel complete
now you're in your seat
the film's a treat
and the music is playing on . . .

As you hold her hand
she takes command
kisses you
it's not as you planned
but that's the way to be.

She's got her evening dress
and never looks stressed
that she's blessed
as a queen of less
just as her less is more.

With energy and possibly
the fragility of a diamond ring
you can be but the one you are
the one you are.

## Oh Clarenbridge

Oh Clarenbridge
I can't afford
the antiques that you sell
but I might as well
take a look
I like that little bell!

Oh Clarenbridge
I can't afford
the secrets that you sell
my mistake
I don't need to buy
that beautiful cooking smell!


## Inside Out

Sitting by the fire
your hair is golden
and your eyes glow brighter.

Sitting out in the weather
I never say never again!

## Snapshot

One chance to film the magic -
are your cameras close at hand?
Strange things happen
when you try to understand.
Not only rapids
are hard to catch on film
the fire and the flames
are harder even still.
don't worry about the detail
'cause the detail is too defined
I like to take it simple
the hardest word to refine!


## In the Breeze

Great balls of fireflies!
I see this identified object
in the skies -
move on
move light
gotta credit card
in the pocket
really gonna spend it right!
Most of us don't work
we fight!
If we open ourselves
with trust
maybe we might.

# Spiders

Spiders
basking
in the sun
on pots
on stones
in the garden.

Spiders
moving
gradually
their little legs
soft yet
placed firmly.

# Acknowledgements

To the butterflies
migrating to NYC
We love ya!
To kindred spirit
and the positive media
we love ya!
To the snow tigers
of Siberia
we love ya!
To Bruce Cathie
and cosmic geometry
we love ya!
To family and friends
not forgetting them
we love ya!

## Sense You Us

You get what you want
but you won't save the words
I know me - or so they say?

What d'you wanna be?
Wanna flow like the sea?
What d'you wanna show?
C'mon and let it go.

You can't have the rainbow
without the rain
I think I heard someone
famous say.

Rain sometime
you got a friend in mine
sun sometime
don't waste your time!

# All the Way

Lovin' in the sun
always so much fun
you get yours
I'll get some
lovin' in the sun.

Finding out you're one
always so much to be done
seek and enjoy
seek and enjoy.

All the way.
All the way.


# Sites and Sounds

Oh
got a friend in you
Oh
what we gonna do?

There's roses in the garden
green grass too
c'mon my friend
I wanna drink with you!

## Visitors

Kissing by the stones
we are not alone
like the stone alignments.
We are gifted bronzed arrivals!
Just blowing their own way
on a sacred site day -
Visted a passage grave
remembered those people
had their way
just nice and quiet
we stepped inside
looked around
no need to hide
from this beautiful
ancient time.

## Awesome Power

Lightning flashes
in the rain grey sky
over the hills
I see fork tongue lines.
Awesome power
I'd forgotten how
this weather changes
to it's own natural now.

I look out of the window
open the front door
to the bow there's a cow
to the stern a fern
on the port side
an elegant tree
on the starboard side
another flash is seen.

From this earth base spore
the cycle's complete
rumbles in the distance
away from where we meet
our home is passed
by awesome power
respect to the natural
the age old flow-er

## `Name

What do you know
there's  the snow
what do you feel
here's a seal
what about your past
right now ~
it's not slow or fast
what's your name?
Bet it's not always the same ?!


## Star Paths

Influential spheres
send out to your loving spears.
Rays of cosmic rivers descend
upon us figures
with us they blend.
Changing what we see
if we want to be
aligning all the time
different formations derived.
Star paths in the sky
move on in time
alright.

## Pregnant Seas

Drowsy calm
well being
tolerating monotony?
Hormone
levels up
to give
cool to mums
nature gives
sensitive to female
to heighten for mumship
details and memories
better remembered
as long as not obsessed!?!


## Elemental

Out in the elements
sum wind rain or snow
out with the elements
MBS in flow
in with the elements
see the fire blaze
in or out with the elements
see the fire blaze
in or out with the elements
let your spirits raise.

## The Fragrance of the Lily

The fragrance of the lily
so subtle
yet so bright
the fragrance slipped through me
I'd forgotten
I'd just used sight.

I didn't even try
the smell just came my way
the thoughts of rubbish
that carried me
immediately fell away.

Clear vision head ~ way
the body did feel
the fragrance of the lily
inspired me
to tell this tale!


## Once

The sun is shining
the sky is grey and blue
the calves are mooing
and I Love you!
The gate is open
the streams do run
lush green hillside
today as one.

## Shadow and Light

It's not too day today
and it won't be
too night tonight
just tonight and today
or today and tonight!

## Flies Fly

flies fly
and flies fly
if we were
named after our actions
what name
would be known by?

Flies fly
and flies fly
fish swim
spiders creep
snakes glide
what name
do we speak?
We peep
we pull
are we people?!

## Cosmetic poetry

Designer design me
a way to resign
yourself myself to love.

It's never been missing
not beside
below or above
just in the shadow
of what you make hollow
yet it's full!

Designer decide to
tap this thing
like a well
it's forever full-filling.

## Sleepy Cottage!

From the quite
majestic flow
I see the structure
and beauty
of my home
this home
our home
just a place
shadow and light
peace and motian
120 years standing
gathering and releasing
our vist
loving now
fresh eyes look on.

## He Brews

He who brews
brews alone
she can brew
if she brews
with he
who is alone!


## Total Artisan Too

Big cellar
small sellar
craft shop style
got her hands full
for just a short while
turning the wheel
small light flickers through
she's reshaped another
that makes a few.

## New-Wage Man

Living life to the full
and full of life
take care give it
like a planetary mid-wife.

A new-wage man
or womb-man has to be
the happiest little creature
in this part of the galaxy?!

Drum to the rhythm
the beat around and given free
dominate here and now
for the likes of you and me.

A new-wage man
or womb-man has to see
that a cool creature
is part of this galaxy!?!

## Sun Sun

Sun Sun
it's you today!
The clouds have come
and gone away
sun sun
a gentle touch
we enjoy your rays
so very much.
Sun sun
the candle in the sky
always there
day or night.
Sun sun warms us through
lightbulb, whatever
shining true
sun sun sun
just look this way!

## *Trails of Beauty*

From Hougue Bie on Jersey
to Carnac in Brittany
there's a trail of beauty
left by the people
who loved to be.

Love Love in the sun
flow the feeling all in one
love love in the sun
flow the feeling on.

From Avebury in Wiltshire
to the stones at Arbor Low
there be a trial of beauty
left by the people
who loved to be.

Love love in the sun
flow the feeling all in one
love love like a snail run
show the feeling on.

# Flip Flop

Sittin' on the beach
sand in my hands
sittin' on the beach
sand on my feet
lookin' at the sky
not a cloud in sight
turned around
saw a wave
she'a catching it right.

The pebbles on the beach
are as old as my toes
they wiggle in the water
and roll with the flow.
The shells on the beach
are as young as my nose
like the pebbles in the water
they roll with the flow.

# Amber

Amber
the great antiseptic tree juice
so lovely and so sweet!
Floats in water
like the wood it came from
looks good in a ring
I know -
she's got one!

## Spatial Beach

A celebration
a tourist pilgrimage
to the temple of the sun
recharging
energising
laying a towel down on one!
From coves to groves
from wheels to fields
yes
under the glowing sun.


## On A Levelling

Look at, look at the trees
they just stand so tall
gentle and bold
withstanding many a strom.
Like like Mr Magoo
you can see what you want to
remember the balloon's pace
too much wind
ands it's lost in space
It's so - so
so get your feet on the ground!
be forever growing
in a beautiful sound
like like the stars join hands
so we try to be
you can be famous
without forcing a thing!

## Lagos

The smell of the fresh fruit thrills
and the boats on the water too
they all just sit there waiting
waiting to be moved.
The orange is a ripe one
full of golden sun so sweet
the banana is another one
this one green and not ready to eat.
the seahorse slogan fascinates
on the wall by the bridge
I guess many people see it
walk past
and try to guess what it is ?


## Trans - Actions

Last night I saw the moon shine
today I see the sun
tonight I'll hear the river
flow under the bridge and on.
Sometimes there are changes
the wheel turns on once more
but the ripples of life
won't disturb the heart.

## Once Upon An Early Morn

Are there any more takers
for the view of the rising sun?
The smell of the moment
is only part of the fun
Yet once it is alright
the party's always right
the light that shines
shines for you.
The rising sun is now in view
close your eyes
feel it
know it's true.

## Many Makes

The Jewell that is us
is ours for good
from the lush green grass
to a dusty mountain view
the experience is cool
and the timing is fine
the creatures in the wild
are moving
to the music of life.

# The Overtaker

Senegal is where she's from
now she knows
where she went wrong
LA said it had it all
but in that city
she was fooled.

At closing time
she sweeps the bar
steps into an old red car
shorter hours
on the work
makes her feel really good.

Ready now she's out tonight
look how clean
her fire's bright
things just stored
not hidden away
wear what she needs
from day to day.
Glasses off to her natural way
she feels for what she needs to say
passes round thoughts like sun
shining down on everyone
summer's here spring has gone
from the Equator to the mighty song?!
Autumn's here summer's gone
leaves are changing like her song
spring is here winter's gone
shorts are short and days are long.

## Orange Eve

An orangy time
of warm appreciation
for the summer past
remembering who's been before
recollecting what has passed.

As the lights freely burn
that night
a candle for a loved one.
Ancient wisdom
all in-sight.


## Aromatic Highways

I've got a bird brother
she's got an insect friend
we hear their songs
Live always
she glides along
stream-like pathways.

And so she flies
way up in the sky
and so she flies.

## Whatever The Weather

I was wet today
as I walked in the rain
away I came
from an arcade.
Shopping today
ping me away
to the hills
where I love to be!


## The Love Reaper

This is the way
you know you know
how do you know
before you try what you try?
How do you feel
what you feel you feel?

## Indian

The girl in the red dress
looks pretty fine
she walks into the movie
and talks all the time
it's OK for others
she just whispers in rhyme
about cats and monkeys
and a friend of mine.

After the movie
she walks to a bar
listens to music
and rides home in her car
independently watching
TV tonight
she switches it off
it's her bedtime.

The girl in the head-dress
sips on her wine
her friends at the party
make it on time
talking with Spanish
listening in French
dreaming in Dutch
but global in touch.

# On The Cusp

Raise a glass
of Chilean wine
just enough
for a beautiful time
really not phazed
we can't be wrong
tonight's tonight
music to star
evening song.


# Turned On Too

Getting out and about
to what's about getting out
and even to whats in!
Shop assistant
I hear you say
you're in your job
still out and about today
class assistant
I saw you wave
you're in your place
still in and about today.

## Let's Remember

Telling stories
all night long
listening to
a healing song
Let's remember
release it now
the future's always clear
ready for a beautiful sound.
Circle round
people here
what a story
that's great to hear.

## The Garden Sent Her

Fine with no throne
a queen's own
a carved home
a honeycomb!

The garden sent her
she's not alone
lands on flowers
makin' journies from home.

## Mountain Flower

A tiny flower
a curvaceous little sun
mountain flower
you change by the hour
open or closed
you're a fine little one.


## No Expert Advice!

Life goes forward
without touchin' it
tomorrow comes
without rushin' it.

Laid back in flow
just that cool
open to respond
to all.

Life never runs away
away from view
'cause you and your life
are together and true.

Sometimes the longer way round
is the best way near
to do what's what
to find what's clear.

## The Whorls of Love

The whorls of love
makin' contact
hard to body
soft to body
there's heat
love's energies
forever free
infinite to treat.
Little circles
running with the skin
feels good today
and cool within.